101
RECOGNITION
SECRETS

101
RECOGNITION
SECRETS

Tools for Motivating and Recognizing Today's Workforce

ROSALIND JEFFRIES

Performance Enhancement Group
Chevy Chase, Maryland

Performance Enhancement Books are available at special discounts when
purchased in bulk for premiums and sales promotions, educational and
business use. For more information please contact the Special Sales
Department at the address below:

Performance Enhancement Group
3312 Shirley Lane
Chevy Chase, MD 20815

Jeffries, Rosalind

   101 recognition secrets: tools for motivating and
recognizing today's work force/Rosalind Jeffries.–1st edition

p.cm.

Preassigned LCCN: 95-73001
ISBN: 0-9648444-2-7

1. Management. 2. Motivation. I. Title.

Cover design and illustration by Michael Welch
Interior design by Lisa Bacchini

Printed in the United States of America
10 9 8 7 6 5 4 3 2 1

Table of Contents

Dedication

This book is dedicated to the thousands of employees from the U.S. and abroad who have given me the basis and content for this publication. My sincere hope is that the "secrets" in this document will become customary for managers responsible for creating the environments in which you work. May your organizations become places you look forward to going each day to give your very best.

Thank you!

Acknowledgments

Although words are not enough to acknowledge the many people who helped make this book possible,

Nancy Kuhn, Carolyn Hines, Robert Holland, Veda Ross, Lori Wong for their support and help throughout this project.

Kathy Wall, to whom I am specially indebted, for her help in gathering and summarizing all the extensive data and for helping me to develop a unique approach to recognition trends.

Ellen Weir, who read through draft after draft. With her fresh eyes, she inspired me to explore new directions.

My sister, Sonserae, for keeping me on track when steam was running low and for discussing ideas with me when I needed an "ear."

Linda Lazar Allen, who is everything anyone could wish for in a publicist and more. She believed in the book from its inception and nurtured it every step of the way.

My dear friends and colleagues, who inspired my efforts to improve the workplace environment.

My mother, a true southerner who couldn't believe you have to teach people how important it is to say "thank you."

And most of all, thank you to my daughter, Ashley, and my husband, Charles, for understanding all the times when I was not there.

Foreword

Little acts of kindness go a long way. Whether in the workplace or at home, people will go the extra mile when they feel appreciated. Yet, with the day-to-day stresses in most businesses, many of us fail to incorporate these little acts of appreciation as part of our daily management practices. A while back, I discovered the obvious — even in environments where employee-based values are extolled and substantial efforts are made to put them into practice, there is always a lot more to do — and learn. This book makes the obvious even more so. *101 Recognition Secrets* is all about business and companies directly benefitting from employee's good deeds. But it is also about companies benefitting indirectly when people display a sensitivity to the needs to others, both inside and outside the company. These acts make us human, and valuable ones at that.

The "secrets" in this book are as basic and elemental as fresh air.

They are common sense in nature — coming in the midst of an academic blitz of new insights in the "science" of the management process and better pathways to the "effective organization." That's what makes the book so meaningful. It gives fingertip access to simple recognition techniques that can be easily implemented in your day-to-day routines.

101 Recognition Secrets takes only a few minutes to read, and it is worth each and every nanosecond! You can put elements of it to work immediately after reading it, and I hope you will.

The goal of this book is to spread the word that RECOGNITION IS AN IMPORTANT PART OF GOOD MANAGEMENT PRACTICES. I highly recommend that you add this book to the front end of your management training programs. We did, and our managers are already getting a lot of mileage out of the suggestions.

Robert Holland, Jr.
President & CEO, Ben & Jerry's Homemade, Inc.

To My Readers

For the past several years, we have focused on re-energizing the American workplace. While we have committed to quality and efficiency, we have often overlooked the key players in our national growth — our employees.

Today's workers view salary increases as a given, looking at salary raises as normal and thus expected financial compensation. These employees are demanding credit for their participation and ideas — and they're not waiting for five– and ten–year service awards.

As we move forward in this new era, it is increasingly critical to embrace vigorously what good managers have always known: recognition is a powerful tool for motivating employees.

What Employees Won't Tell You
(But They Told Me!)

This little book of ways to recognize our employees is the product of over 17 years of training and facilitating workshops and seminars in a variety of industries. It was born of listening to employees describe how starved they are for "thank yous," and of managers describing their recognition techniques that have been successful.

In my research, I found that most managers wanted to recognize their employees, but they didn't know how!

The secrets on the following pages are easy, practical and
inexpensive, and they can set the foundation for achieving the
best from each of your employees. It starts with you! I invite
you now to uncover the secrets to unlocking human potential.

—— Rosalind Jeffries

Introduction

All employees believe that they are competent, sometimes
brilliant, in their work and that their contributions have value.
But they need to hear it from us. In my fifteen years of
presenting workshops in various industries, I've frequently
heard comments like this: "We just want to be noticed for our
contributions on a day-to-day basis!" In short, people want to
hear "Thank you!" Seven out of ten employees want more
individual recognition for their performances. In fact,
inadequate recognition, rather than insufficient compensation,
was the most common reason workers gave for quitting.

Most managers do not understand or take advantage of the
power of recognition. Yet, for managers interested in attracting,

retaining and getting the best performances from employees (and who isn't), the significance of recognition is profound. When we take performance for granted and do not recognize individuals on a regular basis, we miss opportunities to enhance productivity. Too often we watch employees perform their jobs well, but fail to comment. Yet, the moment workers fall short of our expectations, we give them our full attention and plenty of advice. Such "red-pencil mentality" imitates the American educational system, which has traditionally emphasized errors by marking them in bright red. Meanwhile, correct answers go unmarked — seemingly unrecognized. In business as well, we tend to pay close attention to the negative and ignore the positive. We call workers into the office only when things have gone wrong. Is it any wonder then that employees often view management as the enemy?

It doesn't have to be this way, however. With professional training and nominal financial investment, managers can learn to exercise recognition appropriately and effectively. On a macro-level, recognition can significantly boost the level of productivity in the workplace. A number of major corporations are proving my point. In companies such as Children's Hospital of Philadelphia, Taco Bell, Motorola, Toyota, Xerox, IBM, Corning, and Ameritech, programs have been successfully implemented to reinforce learning and performance by providing training in how to give recognition. While none of these organizations has had to invest large sums of money in their recognition programs, they are realizing such dramatic benefits as:

- improved productivity
- increased employee pride and morale
- heightened staff creativity
- improved employee recruitment and retention.

In the pages that follow, I've compiled a variety of practical, inexpensive and ready-to-use ideas for how, when and where you can recognize the people who work for you. To fit the busy schedules of most managers, I designed the book as a quick, 17-minute management tool that will help you easily incorporate the power of recognition. The techniques in this book are real — they're based on the responses of more than 10,000 managers and employees I've researched and taught over the last 15 years. The employees come from all sectors of the economy — from Fortune 500 companies to nonprofit organizations, from small and emerging businesses to the public sector.

Recognizing employees is not the panacea for management-employee relations, but it is a large part of reducing grievances, decreasing poor or marginal performance, and increasing productivity. My hope is that this book will prove to be a useful tool for the growing number of managers who realize that an effective recognition program is key to successful supervision. Ideally, accountability for employee recognition should have a place alongside financial planning, quality assurance and day-to-day oversight as a benchmark for successful management. This book is a step toward making that happen.

What Is This Recognition Business About, Anyway?

It's a rare individual who doesn't derive satisfaction from being recognized for a job well done. Put another way, we're all suckers for attention. But the exciting news here is that the right kind of attention can do more than just make us feel good about ourselves and our efforts. For organizations seeking to maintain and strengthen employee morale and at the same time boost productivity and innovation, the right kind of attention can be a powerful motivating tool.

So what exactly is the "right" kind of attention? This may come as a surprise. It is not necessarily money or material rewards. In fact, organizations are discovering that traditional and costly work force motivators, such as promotions, salary increases, bonuses, certificates, gold watches and the like, do not have the same impact they once did. Times have changed, and so have today's workers. Whereas in years gone by people began their careers expecting to remain loyal to one employer, workers in this new generation believe they will have multiple employers during their professional lives. Therefore, they have different priorities. They don't work for the company; they work for themselves. And, while they certainly are interested in earning a fair salary and traditional benefits, today's

Employee's Definition of Recognition:
"A response from someone that makes me feel good about what I am doing, have done or will do."

workers have additional standards by which they rate their jobs. They are looking for ways to balance the challenges of work and home. They want work that provides them with opportunities for professional and personal growth. And they want to feel as though their good ideas and deeds are valued by the organization.

What can you do to let employees know that their efforts are appreciated? How do you show them that you are aware of their priorities? You can recognize them, their ideas, their accomplishments, and their efforts. Recognition is the right kind of attention as well as a powerful motivator. Through recognition, you show your workers that you value them, that you appreciate the job they are doing, and that you care about their well-being. Recognition also helps people measure their

More Specific
Individual Recognition

70%

30%

Qualitative research showed that seven out of ten
employees at all levels said they wanted specific
individual recognition for a job well done.

performance. Unlike compensation — an expected element —
recognition is special, and can leave a lasting impression.
Through a program of providing recognition on a personal, day-
to-day basis, organizations can develop workers who have high
self-esteem. There is ample research showing that confident
workers are more productive, responsible, and creative. And,
recognition costs little to nothing at all!

It's important to take a moment to examine the distinction
between recognition and reward. A reward consists of money or
something of financial value. Rewards are tangible.
Recognition, on the other hand, is an intangible, which may
or may not be accompanied by reward. It has been defined as
"the act of acknowledging, approving or appreciating an
activity or service." Recognition is a vital method for

acknowledging the importance of an individual's or a team's contributions to the organization. Given the tremendous advantages of recognition, you might think that most organizations rely on it to motivate their workers. Think again. According to qualitative research conducted with more than 10,000 employees, 70 percent — that's 7 out of 10 — of those surveyed said they want specific day-to-day recognition of their contributions. People are starving for attention!

More and more human behavior professionals, management consultants, and others have come to focus on the importance of recognition in the work place. This heightened attention has resulted in more organizations understanding the "what" and the "why" of recognition. But many are unsure of the "how" — how can organizations incorporate recognition into the management function? *101 Recognition Secrets* has the answers, providing valuable tips, suggestions, and strategies for using recognition effectively to motivate employees.

Clearly, recognition is worth doing and it's worth doing right. It's not a quick-fix gimmick. Managers must be willing to make a long-term commitment to providing employees with personal recognition on an ongoing basis. Organizations that ignore the new employee's values and the realities of the modern employment relationship will have a tough time improving morale, attracting and retaining top quality employees, and staying competitive in the marketplace.

Why Recognition Is Important in Today's Business Climate

- Reduced staffing levels require that employees assume more responsibility and work with less supervision.
- Employees want to help shape a work life that is purposeful and motivating.

- In uncertain financial times, recognition provides an effective low-cost way of encouraging higher levels of performance.
- Studies show that personal recognition is the most effective form of motivating staff.

- Recognition is an avenue to boost employee moral and respond to an employee's need for approval and acceptance.

- Recognition provides the means to make people feel valued in uncertain, changing times.

Characteristics of Effective Recognition

Timely:

Recognition should be given to an individual as soon as possible after the performance takes place. Immediate recognition is best. Passage of time reduces the effectiveness of recognition.

Proportional:

Don't overdo your recognition for "small stuff." This will make people question your motives. All good performance should be recognized — but in varying degrees.

Sincere:

Insincere recognition is meaningless and can do great harm. Your employees know you better than you think. Be honest and open with them, and let them know you really appreciate their efforts.

Specific:

An employee should be recognized for a specific behavior or behaviors. To merely say, "good job," isn't enough. Specific appreciation, such as "The level of detail you added to the report was extremely useful in making the key decisions," cues the employee on what behaviors should be repeated in the future. Avoid vague phrases.

Individual:

Individuals should be recognized more so than groups. Within a group, individuals make different contributions. To recognize all when perhaps only a few did most of the work is unfair, and may lead to resentment. If you recognize a group, follow the group recognition by individually rewarding those who are deserving.

Personal:

Have your recognition fit the style of the individual being honored whenever possible.

All people are different, i.e., some individuals may like public praise, while others would prefer a private discussion.

Recognition Secrets

Here they are — the little things that make a big difference!
Try these "secrets" or your own variations to let
your employees know you appreciate their work.

Recognition Secrets

Brag Time

Allow time during meetings for staff members to brag about the outstanding job a department employee did on a specific project. Make meetings a celebration of performance.

Main Lobby Photo Displays

Feature outstanding work groups at your organization in a photo and write-up display placed in a highly visible place, such as the main lobby.

Welcoming and Orienting New Employees

Develop alternative ideas for welcoming new employees to your department. For example, place a rose on the newcomer's desk, along with a card saying: "This bud's for you. Thanks for joining our team." In addition, make transition to the department easier for new employees by offering a creative orientation to the department that involves communication to others outside the department.

Birthday Mail

Have managers and employees sign the card and mail it to the honoree's house before the "big" day instead of presenting the standard birthday card at the annual office birthday party.

By Invitation

Recognize employees by inviting them to receive specialized in-house training from upper management.

"We applaud each little success one after another — and the first thing you know, they actually become successful. We praise them to success!"

Mary Kay Ash, CEO
Mary Kay Cosmetics

Farewell Recognition

Take a moment to recognize every departing employee for his/her efforts while working in your organization.

"When people work in a place that cares about them, they contribute a lot more than duty."

Dennis Hayes,
Hayes Microcomputer
Products, Inc.

Employee of the Month News Release

Send a news release to the employee's hometown community newspaper to publish accolades for your "Employee of the Month."

Congratulatory Memo

Write your employee a personal note of congratulations for excellent performance on handling a difficult customer.

Family Appreciation Letter

Send an appreciation letter to an employee's family, thanking family members for their understanding and support when the employee had to put in long hours of overtime.

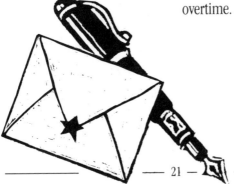

Weekday Surprise

Surprise your staff with something nice on any day of the week for finishing a project, completing inventory, meeting quotas, or managing outside by having a stress-free activity. For example: invite staff to have punch and cookies for 15 minutes to just relax.

Your Substitute

Ask employees to attend meetings in your place when you are not available.

"We blow up the most when we feel unappreciated."

Ava Fluty,
Career Track

Kudos

Webster's Dictionary defines a kudos as an award or honor, a compliment or praise. Develop small but meaningful awards for your employees for doing something "great!"

For example, give Kudos™ candy bars for assisting a very difficult customer.

Timely Feedback

Give your employees feedback—positive or negative—in a timely fashion.

Mentors for Newcomers

Ask an employee to serve as a mentor for a new employee.

Random Acts of Kindness

Give recognition to employees who perform acts of kindness and other good deeds — both on the job and out in the world. When an employee stops to help an elderly person with a heavy package, or assists a stranded motorist, or does something else to help out another human being, we all benefit.

Meet and Greet Those at the Top

Take time to introduce your employees to upper management staff so that effective team building and positive recognition can occur.

Coffee or Lunch with Employees

Have coffee or lunch with an employee or a group of employees whom you do not normally see.

Lack of Public Contact

Plan ways to recognize hard-working employees whose efforts are often unseen because of infrequent public contact. For example, recognize your secretaries with a roll of Lifesavers™ candy for creating an easier filing system.

Supervisory Coffees

Take a short coffee break from a busy schedule to recognize and support an employee for a job well done.

"I'd give more praise."
The Duke of Wellington,
the victor at the
Battle of Waterloo

Top Management Participation

Ask your boss to attend a meeting with your employees during which you recognize both individuals and groups for specific contributions.

Note Performance Improvements

Jot down a message to an employee on your personal stationery, recognizing him or her for better performance on the job.

"The deepest principle in human nature is the craving to be appreciated."

William James,
Philosopher

Department-based Publicity

Inform employees about upcoming events by publicizing them through fliers, table tents and other methods.

Publicize Achievements

Make sure that department and employee achievements are recognized in your company's newsletter.

Good News in Personnel Files

Send letters of commendation to the personnel department for inclusion in employees' personnel folders. And tell the employee that you did this (send a copy and note to employee).

Appreciation Days

Gather your employees to plan a special appreciation day for your department or for certain employees who deserve recognition.

Training Policy

Create a policy stating that at least 16 hours of "training" time per year is to be provided for each employee.

Picture This

Create symbols of a team's work or effort and use this logo on T-shirts or mugs.

Great Beginnings

Briefly attend the first meeting of a quality improvement team to express your appreciation for their involvement.

Pictures

Frame pictures of employees and place them on a wall in the department as a recognition method.

Thank Yous from the Higher-ups

Invite the appropriate senior–level administrator to attend a department meeting to thank employees for their contributions to a department achievement.

Sensitivity

Take time to get to know each of your employees informally so you are sensitive to their special needs and can recognize individuals in ways that meet these needs.

Employee Lounges

Establish a comfortable and appealing area within the department where employees can go when taking a break.

Thank Yous at Project Conclusion

Send a letter to every team member at the conclusion of their work, thanking each for his or her contribution.

Ambassador of the Quarter

Have employees choose an ambassador of the quarter as a method to recognize those who display exemplary performance.

Flexibility in Schedules

Give recognition by allowing employees to work a flexible schedule while still maintaining the normal number of work hours.

Credit When Credit is Due

Remember to give credit to those who have introduced great ideas and completed special projects.

Department Newsletter

Establish a newsletter in your department to inform your employees of current events within the organization.

Become a Working Member

Spend a day "in the trenches," working "hands-on" with the employees in your department.

"You have to be able to listen well if you're going to motivate the people who work for you."

Lee Iacocca

Go Out of Your Way to Recognize Employees

Make a special trip to an employee's office to express appreciation for a job well done.

"Other things being equal, the more immediate the reinforcement, the more powerful it is in terms of strengthening behavior."

Paul L. Brown,
"Managing Behavior on the Job"

Community Involvement

As a department or on behalf of a particular employee, make a donation to a favorite charity. This strengthens staff unity and shows community involvement.

Bright Ideas

Recognize employees by encouraging them to present their own ideas or program possibilities to management.

Off-Site Meetings

Schedule meeting days off-site to provide employees with the opportunity to plan in a different environment. This will give employees further opportunity to contribute to the overall goals of the department.

Bulletin Board

Construct a bulletin board within your department to display such items as letters, memos, pictures, and thank you cards that recognize employees.

Traveling Trophy

Purchase a trophy that travels each month to the department exhibiting the greatest overall performance—behaviors and results—throughout the institution during the previous month.

The Envelope, Please

Draft a thank-you letter to be signed by the next level of management or, when appropriate, by the vice president or general manager.

Highlights

Create a publication that recognizes and rewards employees for their humanistic actions and behaviors.

Field Trip

Take an employee along to visit your company's major supplier.

Policy Changes

As a form of recognition, allow your employees to participate in forming or changing policies that affect the department.

Enter-prize

Establish a suggestion program that rewards employees for their creative ideas regarding cost containment and improved operations.

"There are many ways to honor someone. Just doing it is an asset."
Successful Meetings Magazine.

Rest Stop (or R & R)

Recognize an employee's hard work by presenting him or her with a pillow or a gift certificate for a massage.

International Day of Sharing

Recognize the many cultures and ethnic groups that employees of your organization represent by providing treats that are special to their nationalities.

Recognition Week

Designate a week for
recognizing employees for
their hospitality and hard
work through various
activities and events.

Monthly Luncheon

Have monthly luncheons and
invite guest speakers from
other departments to
exchange ideas and views.
This will also help your staff
gain appreciation for other
staff and departments.

*"We are all suckers
for attention."*

Susan Cook
of the Tom Peters Group

Say Hello, Always

Make a point of always saying "hello" to employees when you pass by their desks or pass them in the hall.

Hot Chocolate for Everyone

Warm up your employees and guests on a cold, winter day with cups of hot chocolate.

Show and Tell

Have employees develop presentations for other employees on "Here Is What I Do."

For Senior Managers Only — Not!

Recognition works at all levels. Senior management should recognize subordinate managers who practice giving recognition to their employees. This is one way to emphasize the importance of recognition as a Good Management Practice.

Popsicle Day

Reward employees for their hard work and dedication with a popsicle on a hot summer day.

Welcome Back Update

Welcome employees back when they return from vacation and bring them up to date.

Create an Award

Create a presidential award such as a pen or plaque.

Message Center

Designate a message center to keep all pertinent memos, letters and information. The center can also serve as a place for staff to record ideas and information to share with one another.

Interior Design

Get employees involved in decorating their office/work area to help create a feeling of ownership.

"People work for money but go the extra mile for recognition, praise and rewards."

Stuart Levine,
CEO Dale Carnegie
and Associates

Employee Involvement

Ask your employees how you can best show your appreciation. What recognition would they like from you?

Department of the Year

Choose a department of the year in each division based on guidelines you establish.

Walking Rounds

Go to your employees instead of them always coming to you. Take "walking rounds" to visit employees at their worksites. This gives you an opportunity to receive feedback on how their jobs are going and to appreciate further their work environment.

Appreciation Sound-Off

Invite an individual into the office for 10 minutes specifically to share an accomplishment. Make sure the appreciation gesture is genuine and specific.

Recognition of Special Events

Make special mention of important, personal employee events such as a marriage, graduation or birth of a child.

"No one rises to low expectations."

Les Brown

Call People By Name

Whenever possible, call the person by name. It has been said that the most welcome word in the English language to each individual is his or her name.

Honor Roll

Create an honor roll of employees recognized by clients, vendors and others for their acts of kindness and support to others on the job.

Community Ties

Create a community service award to be publicized in the local paper as well as internally in the organization.

Recognition at Meetings

Have well-planned meetings.

- Ask an employee to plan and conduct the meeting.

- Invite guest speakers from other departments.

Wish List

For feedback and recognition purposes, have employees complete a wish list of ideas they believe would benefit the department and organization. Implement ideas that are effective and reasonable.

Support-Staff Recognition

Create an award to recognize individuals who are not in the limelight but without whose help a product or project cannot be accomplished.

Employee of the Month

Develop an employee of the month program with special recognition given by top administrators in the institution. Also, include special, creative, inexpensive gifts for the recognized employees.

Courtesy Time Off

Grant employees a day or two of leave for special, personal events in their lives.

"No act of kindness, no matter how small, is ever wasted."

Aesop, *Fables*

Help Your Employees Understand the Big Picture

Help your employees see and understand the "Big Picture." Arrange to have employees in your department visit another work area that is impacted by their work. Allow the employees to plan the visit and explore how their product fits in the overall scheme of things.

Year-in-Review

Produce a year-in-review booklet with pictures or plan a celebration to highlight your employees' proudest achievements of the year.

Staff Development

Recognize and encourage your staff members by allowing them to attend workshops, seminars and other functions. Give special assignments to people who have shown interest and initiative.

Monthly Talk Sessions

Energize your staff with monthly talk sessions. Allow approximately 20 minutes as an agenda item to have employees talk about what's going well, what's not going well and what help they need from you.

Accentuate the Positive

Managers should tell people what they have done right — not just point out mistakes — on a day-to-day basis.

Cross-Department Recognition

Contact another employee's supervisor to inform him or her of the employee's positive behavior and performance in your presence.

Trading Places

When possible, have an employee spend a day trading responsibilities with another employee to see what it is like to have "the shoe on the other foot."

Growth Factors

Recognize an employee who has mastered a new skill or shown professional growth by giving him or her a plant.

Cross-Training

Give your employees the opportunity to develop additional skills and gain appreciation for other employees' responsibilities through cross-training.

"People hear what we say, but they see what we do. And seeing is believing."
Al Lucia, co-author,
Walk the Talk

Help Employees to Be in the Know

Share information from

- Other meetings you attend within the company

- Journals you read

- Professional meetings

Grand Plans

Present an employee with a $100,000™ candy bar in recognition of a grand idea.

"Giving people a chance to be 'visible' for their work and accomplishments is the smartest thing a manager can do to motivate them."

Bits and Pieces,
a monthly publication of
The Economics Press, Inc.

Logos

Involve employees in creating a logo or symbol that represents your department's work to the organization. This logo can be used on T-shirts, memos or in any departmental activity.

Drumming Up Support

Recognize individuals who lead groups, projects or exercises by making them "Honorary Drum Majors." Give each a baton to make the title complete.

Express Appreciation

- In words

- With a smile

Thanks for Working Overtime

Write a thank you note to an employee for putting in extra time in the workplace.

Day-to-Day Thank Yous

Thank your employees daily through letters, notes or personal comments for something positive they've done.

Thanks to Your Boss

Express thanks to your boss when he or she has done something well or helpful to you.

Employee-to-Employee Thank Yous

Visit a fellow employee personally or send a note or letter saying thank you for the help, for the kind word of encouragement.

"Praising all alike is praising none."

John Gay, *Epistles*

Thank You in Rough Times

Take a moment to tell your employees "thank you" personally for a specific task completed during a period of heavy workload.

Thank You Goody Baskets

Distribute a basket of candies or other goodies to employees in your department or section to show your appreciation for something specific.

Thank You Boutonniere

Recognize an employee's positive performance and exemplary workplace behavior with a boutonniere or flower to brighten up his or her day.

Quality Efforts

Cite extraordinary efforts that result in quality performance in the company newsletter or bulletin board.

"What really flatters a man is that you think him worth flattering."
George Bernard Shaw

Team Day

Set aside a day for teams in cross-functional departments to present their results and processes to one another.

Seek Input

Ask employees for their ideas and feedback. Simply asking people for more input is a flattering form of recognition.

Certificates for Using Training

Present certificates to employees who successfully use rather than simply complete training.

"The only justification for looking down on someone is to pick them up."
Jesse Jackson

Building Bridges

Encourage staff members to recognize each other's contributions by verbally thanking one another and creating their own forms of recognition.

"Star" Performers

Feature an employee who has been an overall quality performer on the job in the organization newsletter.

Exemplary Customer Service

Reward employees who demonstrate exemplary customer service through:

- Letter

- Lunch certificate

- Newsletter story

- Upper Management acknowledgment

- Gift Certificate for a Pedicure/Manicure, etc.

(This is an opportunity for the employee to receive customer service)

Grace Under Pressure

Recognize an employee who handles a stressful situation particularly well with a certificate or special award.

Anniversary Date

Commemorate notable anniversaries of service (such as 5, 10, 20 years) to the company by sending the employee a card of congratulations.

"When you are looking for obstacles, you can't find opportunities."
Janet Cheatham Bell

Feedback from Boss

Tell employees when they've done a good job at the time of the event.

15 Ways
to Get Rid of Your Staff

Employee turnover lowers morale, efficiency, production,
and certainly profits. You're more likely to keep workers
if you understand why they're often prompted to quit—
that is, if you learn what *not* to do!

15 Ways
to Get Rid of Your Staff

1 **Never**
ask, "How are you?"

2 **Never**
say, "Thank you."

3 **Never**
take the time to listen.

4 **Never**
acknowledge an
employee's strengths.

5 **Never**
have staff meetings.

6 **Never**
have conferences except
for evaluation purposes.

7 **Never**
acknowledge a job
well-done.

8 Never
change job routine
(if possible).

9 Never
emphasize "People Skills";
only task-oriented skills.

10 Never
ask for input when
decisions are being made.

11 Never
make a person feel
important.

12 Never
get employee
commitment.

13 Never
show empathy.

14 Never
acknowledge professional
development.

15 Never
give credit when credit is
due to an individual.

What Workers Want

The best way to find out what workers want is to ask them!
That way, you can tailor your recognition to
their specific desires. The following pages contain sample
questions and responses from a survey of employees
at a variety of companies.

For What Do You Want to Be Recognized ?

- Prompt attendance

- Providing over and above customer service

- Longevity

- Consistently providing good work

- Dealing with difficult situations (grace under pressure)

- Initiating new ideas

- Taking on specific projects; job-related work

- Paying attention to detail

- Birthday, anniversary recognition

- Covering shifts for other staff members

- Offering assistance to coworkers

- Sacrificing personal time to get the job done

- Working well outside your team

- Making decisions and demonstrating leadership when boss is gone

What Kinds Of Recognition Would You Like To Receive?

- Personal note of thanks

- Letter for personnel file

- Spoken thank you

- Gift certificates

  - to a mall

  - for dinner out for two

- Free lunch

- Movie/concert/play/ event tickets

- Birthday off without using leave

- Recognition of coworkers

- On department bulletin board

- Recognize the team or department at staff meeting

- Savings Bond

- Plaque or certificate

- Credits toward catalog gift

- Achievement acknowledged at staff meetings

- Pin for ID Badge

- Extra lunch time

- Car washed

- Goody bag with candy, treats, and stickers

- Meal by chef

How Would You Like To Receive Your Recognition?

- At staff meeting-department meeting

- Interoffice mail (memo, letter, or e-mail, with a copy to my personnel file)

- One-on-one with a handshake and smile

- Immediately!

- Personal recognition on my specific shift from management

- Ongoing verbal messages

- Posted on a department bulletin board

- Personal handwritten notes

- At the beginning of my shift
- Surprise department party
- Recognition banquet
- Performance evaluation

- Quietly!
- Poster, banner
- Department picnic
- Individual luncheon

How Do You Not Wish To Be Recognized?*

- No sarcasm, unflattering or humorous awards

- Not exclusively in evaluation!

- Not long after the event

- Not by form letter sent to my home

- Not with vague generalities such as "good job!"

- Not in any form that includes the word "but"

- Not in print without my permission

- No gimmicks

- Not with mass department party to use up honor fund money

- Not with a display present (such as flowers) when there's nowhere to display it!

*Note: Some of the same responses also appear on the list of how employees do wish to be recognized, emphasizing this fact: Effective recognition must be tailored to the recipient!

Recognition Essentials

You can add effective employee recognition
to your managerial responsibilities more easily
by keeping these basic themes in mind.

Recognition Essentials

Remember:
The most desired recognition is a simple, genuine, spoken "thank you!"

•

Providing recognition costs little.

•

Giving meaningful recognition takes little time.

•

Recognition must be tailored to the individual.

•

•

Getting to know your employees and finding out what they think is important will enable you to provide unique and effective recognition.

•

It's important that you be sensitive to the special recognition needs of shy and private people.

•

Incorporating positive recognition may require a change in your management style.

•

Practice makes giving recognition easier.

•

Watching and listening to others give recognition
is an excellent way to learn.

•

Encouraging peer recognition is an
important part of the process.

•

The recognition methods you use should fit your personality
and become natural and comfortable with practice.

•

The best way to find out what employees want is to ask them!

•

Missed Opportunities

Employees frequently complain that management doesn't appreciate their efforts. Here are ways managers might take advantage of opportunities and avoid complaints.

"I worked successfully on a project for six months, but received no recognition when I presented it. My supervisor just grabbed my report without even thanking me!"

Give verbal recognition to employee in front of peers.

"We always make a ceremony of celebrating birthdays in the department, including the manager's. Sometimes she sends individual employees cards on birthdays, but when mine came, she must have forgotten it."

•

Know when birthdays of all employees are. Acknowledge or celebrate them consistently.

"When I first started working here, nobody welcomed me or introduced me to other employees. I felt invisible!"

•

Greet new employee with small sign, supplies, banner, breakfast. Introduce to other employees and office.

"The computer system I designed and set up for our department is running great. But the manager hasn't even said thank you!"

•

Give verbal compliment. (Often only negative glitches in a computer system receive attention!)

"I coordinated a successful project involving four departments in the corporation. They all got acknowledged at a big meeting, but I didn't get as much as a thanks for making everything work."

•

Send a memo or verbally recognize employee in front of peers.

"When my boss was stuck with a problem she couldn't solve, I helped her come up with a perfect solution. If she appreciated my help, she didn't bother to tell me!"

•

Send out note, flowers.

"At the board meeting, all we heard were the few negative things about our presentation, not the many positives!"

•

Avoid "red pencil" recognition by highlighting positives instead.

"When our program was evaluated, the vice president reported the results to the managers but didn't even let us know how we fared."

•

Talk directly to the staff about results concerning their program.

"I spent weeks of my own time developing a workshop that wasn't even part of my job responsibility. The boss didn't recognize my contribution."

•

Acknowledge in weekly staff meeting. Give time off.

"When our center was highlighted in a feature article in the newsletter, only the manager was mentioned. They left out our entire resident staff!"

•

Give employees credit. Provide picture for recognition.

"Our department staff worked through lunch breaks and overtime for two weeks so we could meet a critical deadline. We saved the boss on this one, but didn't get so much as a thanks!"

•

Give immediate and specific verbal feedback for an individual's role in crisis.

Phrases to Rephrase

To be most effective, recognition should be individualized.
Review the following examples which demonstrate how vague
comments can be changed to meaningful, specific statements
of appreciation.

Good Job!

•

**I really appreciate the fact
that you paid specific
attention to line #9 in the
billing application. It brought
us an additional $20,000!**

Well done!

•

**I realize it took you some
hard work and extra time
to collect and organize all
that data by Thursday. I
really appreciate it, Jean.**

You're a team player.

•

Lauren, thanks for taking the lead in providing us with information on our new computer system capabilities. With your help, the team saved over $1,000 on training and documentation.

You are a real life saver!

•

Thanks for taking over for Lori when she got called out on emergency. I know adding four more patients to your load isn't easy.

Thanks for your help!

Good show!

•

•

I truly appreciate your getting the safety manual done while I was gone. Let me buy you lunch!

Thanks, Melissa, for taking the initiative to make arrangements for the move. Your attention to the packing, carpet selection, and follow-up with vendors was critical to a smooth remodeling of the office.

We couldn't function without you!

•

Thanks for putting out the most complete, professional, and readable quarterly report we've ever had!

I appreciate you.

•

Thanks a million, Charles, for getting Mike to drive Mr. Clinton to the airport. I'm sorry I forgot to give you the reservation.

Ways to Recognize
Marginal Performers

Ask yourself:

- Why is the employee a marginal performer?

- What can I do to help rectify the problem?

- How do I provide recognition?

Ask the employee:

- What do you like about what you did?

- What would you do differently if you could redo the task?

- What help do you need from me?

Typical causes for marginal performers are:

- Lack of clarity regarding satisfying performance

- Employee not challenged

- Personal problems

- Lack of proper orientation to the job

- Substance abuse

- Lack of adequate skills

Tips for Working With Marginal Employees

- Remember that every person has different wants, needs, and expectations

- Assess each situation individually and act accordingly

- Provide specific training

- Redefine job

- Seek assistance form Employee Assistance Program (EAP)

- Do skills assessment

- Provide career development/planning

- Provide opportunity for growth

- Ask for employee's input

- Involve employee in decision making

- Notice and acknowledge positive behavior.

Four-step Recognition Planning Sheet

Identify one person or team that you would like to recognize.
Review the 4-step planning sheet for each person or team.

Name:

1. Describe in detail which behavior(s) you will acknowledge.

2. How does the behavior impact the person or team, the
   department, and the organization?

3. Where will the recognition activity or celebration take place?

4. What words will you use to express appreciation for the
   specific behavior(s) described above?

About the Author

Rosalind (Roz) Jeffries is a nationally known and respected managment consultant and speaker specializing in the areas of recognition systems and processes. During her seventeen years as an internal and external human resources development professional, Jeffries has developed a process that directly links recognition to the business practices in organizations. Her book and workshops are based on the results of a three-year project examining the power of recognition with over 10,000 managers and employees in organizations of all types and sizes, from Fortune 500 companies to small businesses. Through interviews, workshops and focus groups, Jeffries identified the most effective (and ineffective) forms of recognition for organizations.

Jeffries' work has led to speaking appearances at numerous conferences across the country, including American Society for Training and Development, Best of America, Positive Employee Practices Institute, Potentials in Marketing, National Association of Healthcare Executives and International Quality and Productivity Center. Jeffries has trained thousands of managers and has helped implement successful recognition programs at some of the nation's leading organizations, including International Business Machines, Children's Hospital of Philadelphia, Forest City Auto Parts, US Department of Commerce, Kaiser Permanente and US Postal Service.

Her company, Performance Enhancement Group, is a full-service, performance-based organization, working in partnership with other organizations to enhance current skills

and develop new ones to meet employees' professional needs,
coupled with the needs of the organization. Workshops and
services focus on four critical needs: Business Needs,
Performance Needs, Training, and Work Environment Needs.

Workshops available include:

- Effective Meeting
  Management

- Employee Motivation

- Management Development

- Managing Problem
  Employees

- Performance Management
  Processes

- Supervisory Skills

- Team Building and
  Development

- Recognition Systems

- Conflict Management
- Hiring the Best...Keeping the Best
- Customer Service Excellence

- Professional Office Practices
- Communication Skills
- Giving and Taking Criticism
- Communicating with the Boss

If you would like to receive additional information on workshops and sessions, or would like to order additional copies of *101 Recognition Secrets*, please contact:

Performance Enhancement Group
3312 Shirley Lane
Chevy Chase, MD 20815
301-654-8449
Fax 301-654-2039